spot

BABY ANIMALS

I0888901

BABY HIPPOS

by K.C. Kelley

AMICUS

school

mouth

Look for these words and pictures as you read.

nose

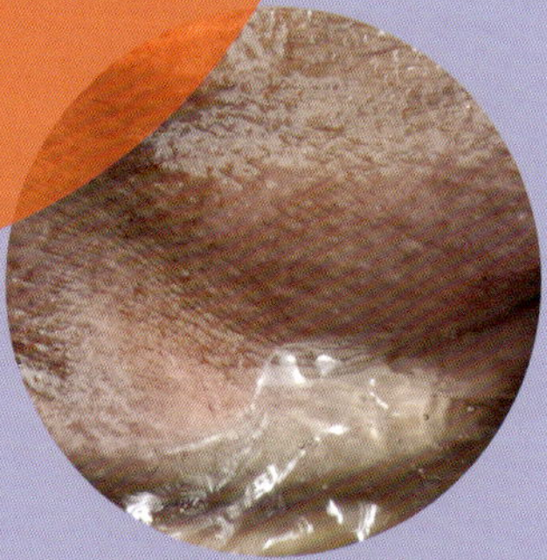

skin

What is that?
It's a baby hippo!

Baby hippos live in Africa.
A baby hippo is called a calf.
They are born in water.

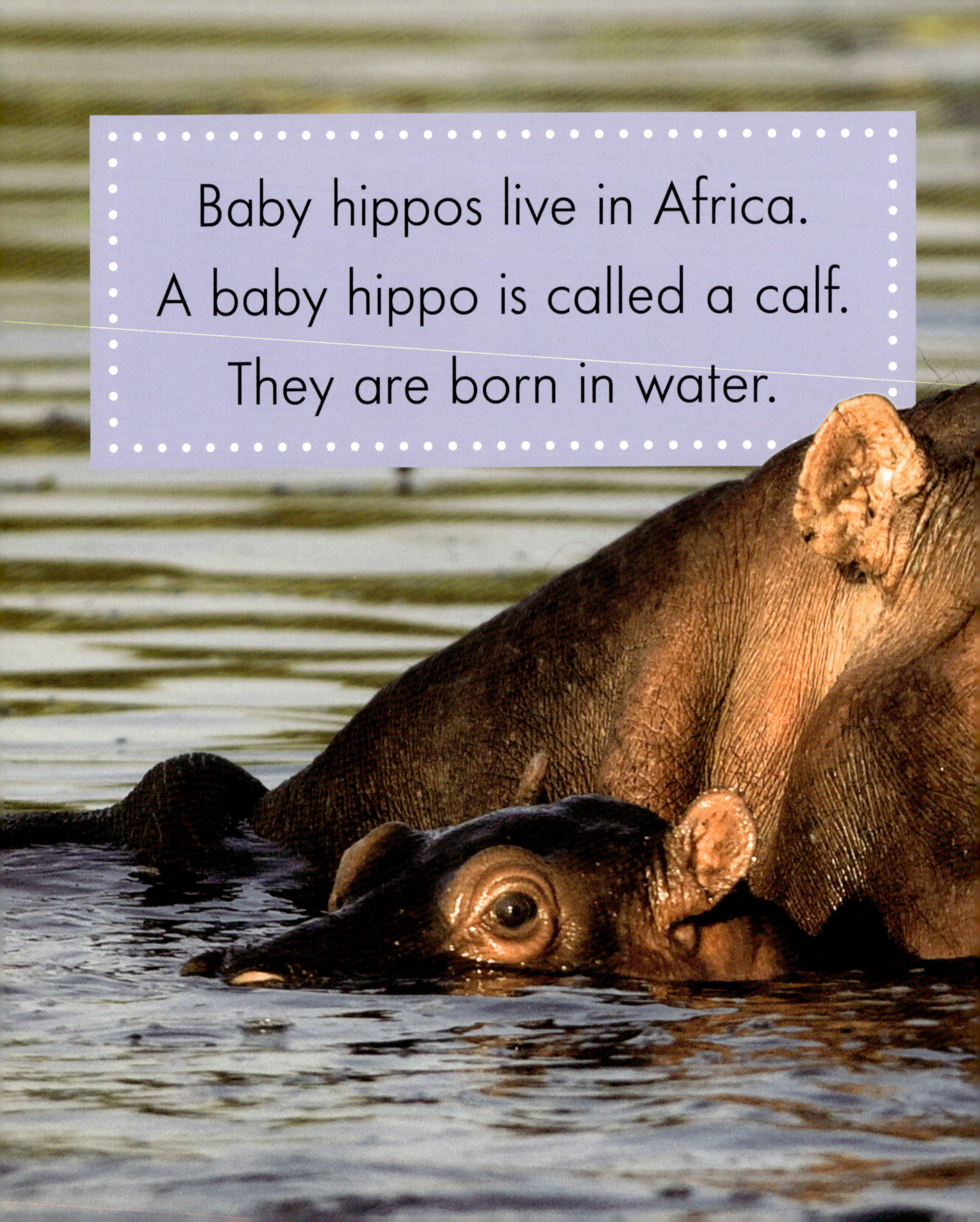

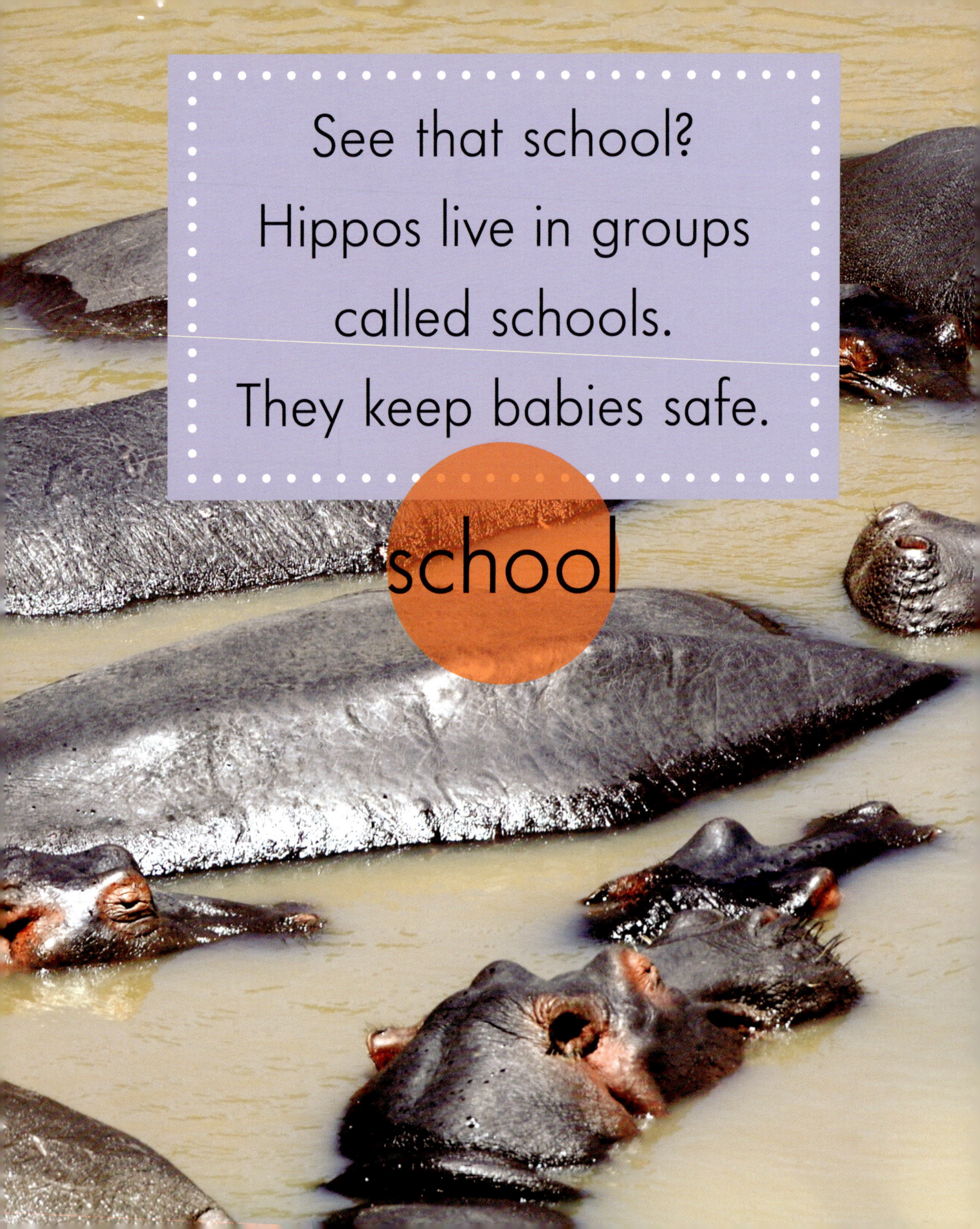

See that school?
Hippos live in groups
called schools.
They keep babies safe.

school

mouth

Look at its mouth. Baby hippos drink their mother's milk. They munch on grass.

nose

See the calf's nose?
The nose closes underwater.

skin

Look at the hippo's skin.
Its skin is oily.
The oil keeps it safe
from the sun.

This baby hippo climbs onto its mother's back. Time to rest!

school

mouth

Did you find?

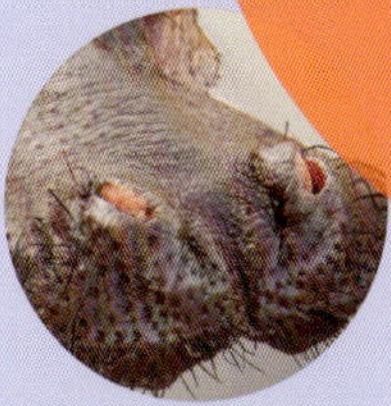

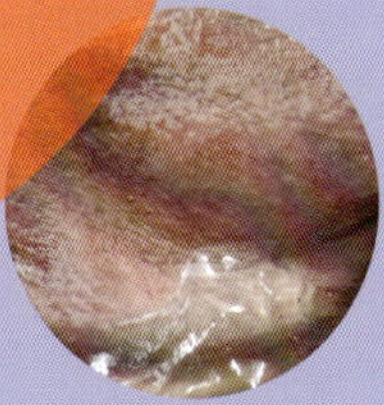

nose

skin

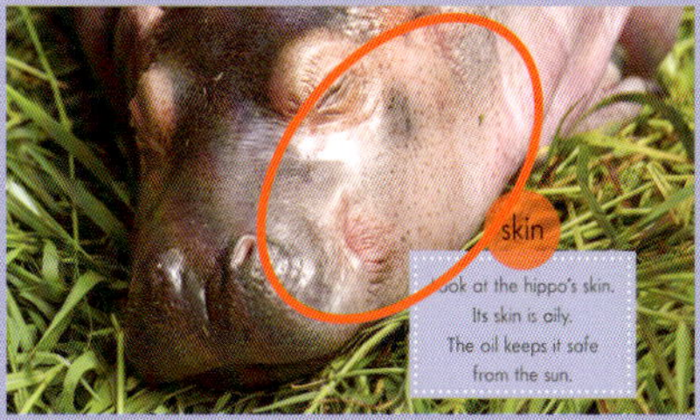

Amicus Readers and Amicus Ink are imprints of Amicus
P.O. Box 1329, Mankato, MN 56002
www.amicuspublishing.us

Copyright © 2018 Amicus.
International copyright reserved in all countries.
No part of this book may be reproduced in any form
without written permission from the publisher.

Cataloging-in-Publication Data is on file with the Library of Congress
ISBN 978-1-68151-322-5 (library binding)
ISBN 978-1-68152-256-2 (paperback)
ISBN 978-1-68151-336-2 (eBook)

Printed in China

HC 10 9 8 7 6 5 4 3 2 1
PB 10 9 8 7 6 5 4 3 2 1

Megan Peterson, editor
Deb Miner, series designer
Patty Kelley, book designer
Producer/Photo Research:
Shoreline Publishing Group LLC

Photos:
Cover: Colombo Nicolo/
Shutterstock.
Inside: Dreamstime.com:
Anyaivanova 1, Znm 2tl, 6,
Zuzana Randlova 2tr, Vesna
Njagulj 2bl, Michiel Bosch 2br,
Lianquan Yu 3, Sergey Uryadnikov
4, Pop2nix 12, Iseelee 14.
Minden Pictures: Cyril Ruoso 8.
Shutterstock: Lumen-digital 10.